Encyclical Letter

ON
HUMAN WORK

Laborem Exercens

On the Ninetieth Anniversary of
Rerum Novarum

Addressed by the Supreme Pontiff
John Paul II

To His Venerable Brothers in the Episcopate
to the Priests
to the Religious Families
to the Sons and Daughters of the Church
and to All Men and Women of Good Will

Pauline
ST. PAUL BOOKS & MEDIA

Vatican Translation from
Vatican Polyglot Press

Printed and published in the U.S.A. by St. Paul Books & Media, 50 St. Paul's Avenue, Boston, MA 02130

St. Paul Books & Media is the publishing house of the Daughters of St. Paul, an international congregation of women religious serving the Church with the communications media.

CONTENTS

I

INTRODUCTION

II

WORK AND MAN

III

CONFLICT BETWEEN LABOR AND CAPITAL
IN THE PRESENT PHASE OF HISTORY

IV

RIGHTS OF WORKERS

V

ELEMENTS FOR A SPIRITUALITY OF WORK

Venerable Brothers and dear sons and daughters,
Greetings and the apostolic blessing.

Through work man must earn his daily bread[1] and contribute to the continual advance of science and technology and, above all, to elevating unceasingly the cultural and moral level of the society within which he lives in community with those who belong to the same family. And work means any activity by man, whether manual or intellectual, whatever its nature or circumstances; it means any human activity that can and must be recognized as work, in the midst of all the many activities of which man is capable and to which he is predisposed by his very nature, by virtue of humanity itself. Man is made to be in the visible universe an image and likeness of God Himself,[2] and he is placed in it in order to subdue the earth.[3] From the beginning therefore he is *called to work*. *Work is one of the characteristics that distinguish* man from the rest of creatures, whose activity for sustaining their lives cannot be called work. Only man is capable of work, and only man works, at the same time by work occupying his existence on earth. Thus work bears a particular mark of man and of humanity, the mark of a person operating within a community of persons. And this mark decides its interior characteristics; in a sense it constitutes its very nature.

I
INTRODUCTION

1. Human Work
on the Ninetieth Anniversary
of "Rerum Novarum"

Since May 15 of the present year was the *ninetieth anniversary* of the publication by the great Pope of the "social question," Leo XIII, of the decisively important encyclical which begins with the words *Rerum novarum*, I wish to devote this document to *human work* and, even more, to *man* in the vast context of the reality of work. As I said in the Encyclical *Redemptor hominis*, published at the beginning of my service in the See of St. Peter in Rome, man "is the primary and fundamental way for the Church,"[4] precisely because of the inscrutable mystery of redemption in Christ; and so it is necessary to return constantly to this way and to follow it ever anew in the various aspects in which it shows us all the wealth and at the same time all the toil of human existence on earth.

Work is one of these aspects, a perennial and fundamental one, one that is always relevant and constantly demands renewed attention and decisive witness. Because fresh *questions* and *problems* are always arising, there are always fresh hopes, but also fresh fears and threats, connected with this basic dimension of human existence: man's life is built up every day from work, from work it derives its specific dignity, but at the same time work contains the unceasing measure of human toil and suffering, and also of the harm and injustice which penetrate deeply into social life within individual nations and on the international level. While it is true that man eats the bread produced by the work of his hands[5]—and this means not only the daily bread by which his body keeps alive but also the bread of science and progress, civilization and culture—it is also a perennial truth that he eats this bread by *"the sweat of his face,"*[6] that is to say, not only by personal effort and toil but also in the midst of many tensions, conflicts and crises, which, in relationship with the reality of work, disturb the life of individual societies and also of all humanity.

We are celebrating the ninetieth anniversary of the Encyclical *Rerum novarum* on the eve of new developments in technological, economic and political conditions which, according to many experts, will influence the world of work and production no less than the industrial revolution of the last century. There are many factors of a general nature: the widespread introduction of automation into many spheres of production, the increase in the cost of energy and raw materials, the growing realization that the heritage of nature is limited and that it is being intolerably polluted, and the emergence on the political scene of peoples who, after centuries of subjection, are demanding their rightful place among the nations and in international decision-making. These new conditions and demands will require a reordering and adjustment of the structures of the modern economy and of the distribution of work. Unfortunately, for millions of skilled workers these changes may perhaps mean unemployment, at least for a time, or the need for retraining. They will very probably involve a reduction or a less rapid increase in material well-being for the more developed countries. But they can also bring relief and hope to the millions who today live in conditions of shameful and unworthy poverty.

It is not for the Church to analyze scientifically the consequences that these changes may have on human society. But the Church considers it her task always to call attention to the dignity and rights of those who work, to condemn situations in which that dignity and those rights are violated, and to help to guide the above-mentioned changes so as to ensure authentic progress by man and society.

2. In the Organic Development of the Church's Social Action and Teaching

It is certainly true that work, as a human issue, is at the very center of the "social question" to which, for almost a hundred years, since the publication of the above-mentioned encyclical, the Church's teaching and the many undertakings connected with her apostolic mission have been especially directed. The present reflections on work are not intended to follow a different line, but rather to be in organic connection with the whole tradition of this teaching and activity. At the same time, however, I am making them, according to the indication in the Gospel, in order to bring out *from the heritage of the Gospel "what is new and what is old."*[7] Certainly, work is part of "what is old"—as old as man and his life on earth. Nevertheless, the general situation of man in the modern world, studied and analyzed in its various aspects of geography, culture and civilization, calls for the discovery of the *new meanings of human work.* It likewise calls for the formulation of the *new tasks* that in this sector face each individual, the family, each country, the whole human race, and, finally, the Church herself.

During the years that separate us from the publication of the Encyclical *Rerum novarum*, the social question has not ceased to engage the Church's attention. Evidence of this are the many documents of the Magisterium issued by the Popes and by the Second Vatican Council, pronouncements by individual Episcopates, and the activity of the various centers of thought and of practical apostolic initiatives, both on the international level and at the level of the local Churches. It is difficult to list here in detail all the manifestations of the commitment of the Church and of Christians in the social question, for they are too numerous. As a result of the Council, the main coordinating center in this field is the *Pontifical Commission Justice and Peace,* which has corresponding bodies within the individual Bishops' Conferences. The name of this institution is very significant. It indicates that the social question must be dealt with in its whole complex dimension. Commitment to justice must be closely linked with commitment to peace in the modern world. This twofold commitment is certainly supported by the painful experience of the two great world wars which in the course of the last ninety years have convulsed many European countries and, at least partially, countries in other continents. It is supported, especially since the Second

8

World War, by the permanent threat of a nuclear war and the prospect of the terrible self-destruction that emerges from it.

If we follow the *main line of development of the documents* of the supreme Magisterium of the Church, we find in them an explicit confirmation of precisely such a statement of the question. The key position, as regards the question of world peace, is that of John XXIII's Encyclical *Pacem in terris.* However, if one studies the development of the question of social justice, one cannot fail to note that, whereas during the period between *Rerum novarum* and Pius XI's *Quadragesimo anno* the Church's teaching concentrates mainly on the just solution of the "labor question" within individual nations, in the next period the Church's teaching widens its horizon to take in the whole world. The disproportionate distribution of wealth and poverty and the existence of some countries and continents that are developed and of others that are not call for a leveling out and for a search for ways to ensure just development for all. This is the direction of the teaching in John XXIII's Encyclical *Mater et magistra*, in the Pastoral Constitution *Gaudium et spes* of the Second Vatican Council, and in Paul VI's Encyclical *Populorum progressio.*

This trend of development of the Church's teaching and commitment in the social question exactly corresponds to the objective recognition of the state of affairs. While in the past *the "class" question* was especially highlighted as the center of this issue, in more recent times it is *the "world" question* that is emphasized. Thus, not only the sphere of class is taken into consideration but also the world sphere of inequality and injustice, and, as a consequence, not only the class dimension but also the world dimension of the tasks involved in the path towards the achievement of justice in the modern world. A complete analysis of the situation of the world today shows in an even deeper and fuller way the meaning of the previous analysis of social injustices; and it is the meaning that must be given today to efforts to build justice on earth, not concealing thereby unjust structures but demanding that they be examined and transformed on a more universal scale.

3. The Question of Work, the Key to the Social Question

In the midst of all these processes—those of the diagnosis of objective social reality and also those of the Church's teaching in the sphere of the complex and many-sided social question—*the question of human work* naturally appears many times. This issue is, in a way, a *constant factor* both of social life and of the Church's teaching. Furthermore, in this teaching, attention to the question goes back much further than the last ninety years. In fact the Church's social teaching finds its source in Sacred Scripture, beginning with the book of Genesis and especially in the Gospel and the writings of the Apostles. From the beginning it was part of the Church's teaching, her concept of man and life in society, and, especially, the social morality which she worked out according to the needs of the different ages. This traditional patrimony was then inherited and developed by the teaching of the Popes on the modern "social question," beginning with the Encyclical *Rerum novarum*. In this context, study of the question of work, as we have seen, has continually been brought up to date while maintaining that Christian basis of truth which can be called ageless.

While in the present document we return to this question once more—without however any intention of touching on all the topics that concern it—this is not merely in order to gather together and repeat what is already contained in the Church's teaching. It is rather in order to highlight—perhaps more than has been done before—the fact that human work is *a key*, probably *the essential key*, to the whole social question, if we try to see that question really from the point of view of man's good. And if the solution—or rather the gradual solution—of the social question, which keeps coming up and becomes ever more complex, must be sought in the direction of "making life more human,"[8] then the key, namely human work, acquires fundamental and decisive importance.

II
WORK AND MAN

4. In the Book of Genesis

The Church is convinced that work is a fundamental dimension of man's existence on earth. She is confirmed in this conviction by considering the whole heritage of the many sciences devoted to man: anthropology, palaeontology, history, sociology, psychology and so on; they all seem to bear witness to this reality in an irrefutable way. But the source of the Church's conviction is above all the revealed word of God, and therefore what is *a conviction of the intellect* is also *a conviction of faith*. The reason is that the Church—and it is worthwhile stating it at this point—believes in man: she *thinks of man* and addresses herself to him *not only* in the light of historical experience, not only with the aid of the many methods of scientific knowledge, but in the first place in the light of the revealed word of the living God. Relating herself to man, she seeks *to express* the eternal *designs* and transcendent *destiny* which *the living God*, the Creator and Redeemer, has linked with him.

The Church finds *in the very first pages of the book of Genesis* the source of her conviction that work is a fundamental dimension of human existence on earth. An analysis of these texts makes us aware that they express—sometimes in an archaic way of manifesting thought—the fundamental truths about man, in the context of the mystery of creation itself. These truths are decisive for man from the very beginning, and at the same time they trace out the main lines of his earthly existence, both in the state of original justice and also after the breaking, caused by sin, of the Creator's original covenant with creation in man. When man, who had been created "in the image of God...male and female,"[9] hears the words: "Be fruitful and *multiply, and fill the earth and subdue it,*"[10] even though these words do not refer directly and explicitly to work, beyond any doubt they indirectly indicate it as an activity for man to carry out in the world. Indeed, they show its very deepest essence. Man is the image of God partly through the mandate received from his Creator to subdue, to dominate, the earth. In carrying out this mandate, man, every human being, reflects the very action of the Creator of the universe.

Work understood as a "transitive" activity, that is to say an activity beginning in the human subject and directed towards an external object, presupposes a specific dominion by man over "the earth," and in its turn it confirms and develops this dominion. It is clear that the term "the earth" of which the biblical text speaks is to be understood in the first place as that fragment of the visible universe that man inhabits. By extension, however, it can be understood as the whole of the visible world insofar as it comes within the range of man's influence and of his striving to satisfy his needs. The expression "subdue the earth" has an immense range. It means all the resources that the earth (and indirectly the visible world) contains and which, through the conscious activity of man, can be discovered and used for his ends. And so these words, placed at the beginning of the Bible, *never cease to be relevant.* They embrace equally the past ages of civilization and economy, as also the whole of modern reality and future phases of development, which are perhaps already to some extent beginning to take shape, though for the most part they are still almost unknown to man and hidden from him.

While people sometimes speak of periods of "acceleration" in the economic life and civilization of humanity or of individual nations, linking these periods to the progress of science and technology and especially to discoveries which are decisive for social and economic life, at the same time it can be said that none of these phenomena of "acceleration" exceeds the essential content of what was said in that most ancient of biblical texts. As man, through his work, becomes more and more the master of the earth, and as he confirms his dominion over the visible world, again through his work, he nevertheless remains

12

in every case and at every phase of this process within the Creator's original ordering. And this ordering remains necessarily and indissolubly linked with the fact that man was created, as male and female, "in the image of God." This *process* is, at the same time, *universal:* it embraces all human beings, every generation, every phase of economic and cultural development, and *at the same time* it is a process that takes place *within each human being*, in each conscious human subject. Each and every individual is at the same time embraced by it. Each and every individual, to the proper extent and in an incalculable number of ways, takes part in the giant process whereby man "subdues the earth" through his work.

5. Work in the Objective Sense: Technology

This universality and, at the same time, this multiplicity of the process of "subduing the earth" throw light upon human work, because man's dominion over the earth is achieved in and by means of work. There thus emerges the meaning of *work in an objective sense*, which finds expression in the various epochs of culture and civilization. Man dominates the earth by the very fact of domesticating animals, rearing them and obtaining from them the food and clothing he needs, and by the fact of being able to extract various natural resources from the earth and the seas. But man "subdues the earth" much more when he begins to cultivate it and then to transform its products, adapting them to his own use. Thus agriculture constitutes through human work a primary field of economic activity and an indispensable factor of production. Industry in its turn will always consist in linking the earth's riches—whether nature's living resources, or the products of agriculture, or the mineral or chemical resources—with man's work, whether physical or intellectual. This is also in a sense true in the sphere of what are called service industries, and also in the sphere of research, pure or applied.

In industry and agriculture man's work has today in many cases ceased to be mainly manual, for the toil of human hands and muscles is aided by *more and more highly perfected machinery*. Not only in industry but also in agriculture we are witnessing the transformations made possible by the gradual development of science and technology. Historically speaking, this, taken as a whole, has caused great changes in civilization, from the beginning of the "industrial era" to the successive phases of development through new technologies, such as the electronics and the microprocessor technology in recent years.

While it may seem that in the industrial process it is the machine that "works" and man merely supervises it, making it function and keeping it going in various ways, it is also true that for this very reason industrial development provides grounds for reproposing in new ways the question of human work. Both the original industrialization that gave rise to what is called the worker question and the subsequent industrial and post-industrial changes show in an eloquent manner that, even in the age of ever more mechanized "work," *the proper subject of work continues to be man.*

The development of industry and of the various sectors connected with it, even the most modern electronics technology, especially in the fields of miniaturization, communications and tele-communications and so forth, shows how vast is the role of technology, that ally of work that human thought has produced, in the interaction between the subject and object of work (in the widest sense of the word). Understood in this case not as a capacity or aptitude for work, but rather as *a whole set of instruments* which man uses in his work, technology is undoubtedly man's ally. It facilitates his work, perfects, accelerates and augments it. It leads to an increase in the quantity of things produced by work, and in many cases improves their quality. However, it is also a fact that, in some instances, technology can cease to be man's ally and become almost his enemy, as when the mechanization of work "supplants" him, taking away all personal satisfaction and the incentive to creativity and responsibility, when it deprives many workers of their previous employment, or when, through exalting the machine, it reduces man to the status of its slave.

If the biblical words "subdue the earth" addressed to man from the very beginning are understood in the context of the whole modern age, industrial and post-industrial, then they
14

undoubtedly include also *a relationship with technology*, with the world of machinery which is the fruit of the work of the human intellect and a historical confirmation of man's dominion over nature.

The recent stage of human history, especially that of certain societies, brings a correct affirmation of technology as a basic coefficient of economic progress; but, at the same time, this affirmation has been accompanied by and continues to be accompanied by the raising of essential questions concerning human work in relationship to its subject, which is man. These questions are particularly charged with *content and tension of an ethical and social character*. They therefore constitute a continual challenge for institutions of many kinds, for States and governments, for systems and international organizations; they also constitute a challenge for the Church.

6. Work in the Subjective Sense: Man as the Subject of Work

In order to continue our analysis of work, an analysis linked with the word of the Bible telling man that he is to subdue the earth, we must concentrate our attention on *work in the subjective sense*, much more than we did on the objective significance, barely touching upon the vast range of problems known intimately and in detail to scholars in various fields and also, according to their specializations, to those who work. If the words of the book of Genesis to which we refer in this analysis of ours speak of work in the objective sense in an indirect way, they also speak only indirectly of the subject of work; but what they say is very eloquent and is full of great significance.

Man has to subdue the earth and dominate it, because as the "image of God" he is a person, that is to say, a subjective being capable of acting in a planned and rational way, capable of deciding about himself, and with a tendency to self-realization. *As a person, man is therefore the subject of work.* As a person he works, he performs various actions belonging to the work process; independently of their objective content, these actions must all serve to realize his humanity, to fulfill

15

the calling to be a person that is his by reason of his very humanity. The principal truths concerning this theme were recently recalled by the Second Vatican Council in the Constitution *Gaudium et spes*, especially in chapter one, which is devoted to man's calling.

And so this "dominion" spoken of in the biblical text being meditated upon here refers not only to the objective dimension of work but at the same time introduces us to an understanding of its subjective dimension. Understood as a process whereby man and the human race subdue the earth, work corresponds to this basic biblical concept only when throughout the process man manifests himself and confirms himself *as the one who "dominates."* This dominion, in a certain sense, refers to the subjective dimension even more than to the objective one: this dimension conditions *the very ethical nature* of work. In fact there is no doubt that human work has an ethical value of its own, which clearly and directly remains linked to the fact that the one who carries it out is a person, a conscious and free subject, that is to say, a subject that decides about himself.

This truth, which in a sense constitutes the fundamental and perennial heart of Christian teaching on human work, has had and continues to have primary significance for the formulation of the important social problems characterizing whole ages.

The ancient world introduced its own typical differentiation of people into classes according to the type of work done. Work which demanded from the worker the exercise of physical strength, the work of muscles and hands, was considered unworthy of free men, and was therefore given to slaves. By broadening certain aspects that already belonged to the Old Testament, Christianity brought about a fundamental change of ideas in this field, taking the whole content of the Gospel message as its point of departure, especially the fact that the one who, while *being God*, became like us in all things[11] devoted most of the years of His life on earth to *manual work* at the carpenter's bench. This circumstance constitutes in itself the most eloquent "Gospel of work," showing that the basis for determining the value of human work is not primarily the kind of work being done but the fact that the one who is doing it is a person. The sources of the dignity of work are to be sought primarily in the subjective dimension, not in the objective one.

Such a concept practically does away with the very basis of the ancient differentiation of people into classes according to the kind of .work done. This does not mean that, from the objective point of view, human work cannot and must not be rated and qualified in any way. It only means that *the primary basis of the value of work is man himself*, who is its subject. This leads immediately to a very important conclusion of an ethical nature: however true it may be that man is destined for work and called to it, in the first place work is "for man" and not man "for work." Through this conclusion one rightly comes to recognize the preeminence of the subjective meaning of work over the objective one. Given this way of understanding things, and presupposing that different sorts of work that people do can have greater or lesser objective value, let us try nevertheless to show that each sort is judged above all by *the measure of the dignity* of the subject of work, that is to say the person, *the individual who carries it out.* On the other hand, independently of the work that every man does, and presupposing that this work constitutes a purpose—at times a very demanding one—of his activity, this purpose does not possess a definitive meaning in itself. In fact, in the final analysis it is always man who is *the purpose of the work*, whatever work it is that is done by man—even if the common scale of values rates it as the merest "service," as the most monotonous, even the most alienating work.

7. A Threat to the Right Order of Values

It is precisely these fundamental affirmations about work that always emerged from the wealth of Christian truth, especially from the very message of the "Gospel of work," thus creating the basis for a new way of thinking, judging and acting. In the modern period, from the beginning of the industrial age, the Christian truth about work had to oppose the various trends of *materialistic and economistic* thought.

For certain supporters of such ideas, work was understood and treated as a sort of "merchandise" that the worker

—especially the industrial worker—sells to the employer, who at the same time is the possessor of the capital, that is to say, of all the working tools and means that make production possible. This way of looking at work was widespread especially in the first half of the nineteenth century. Since then, explicit expressions of this sort have almost disappeared, and have given way to more human ways of thinking about work and evaluating it. The interaction between the worker and the tools and means of production has given rise to the development of various forms of capitalism—parallel with various forms of collectivism—into which other socioeconomic elements have entered as a consequence of new concrete circumstances, of the activity of workers' associations and public authorities, and of the emergence of large transnational enterprises. Nevertheless, the *danger* of treating work as a special kind of "merchandise," or as an impersonal "force" needed for production (the expression "work force" is, in fact, in common use) *always exists*, especially when the whole way of looking at the question of economics is marked by the premises of materialistic economism.

A systematic opportunity for thinking and evaluating in this way, and in a certain sense a stimulus for doing so, is provided by the quickening process of the development of a onesidedly materialistic civilization, which gives prime importance to the objective dimension of work, while the subjective dimension—everything in direct or indirect relationship with the subject of work—remains on a secondary level. In all cases of this sort, in every social situation of this type, there is a confusion or even a reversal of the order laid down from the beginning by the words of the book of Genesis: *Man is treated as an instrument of production,*[12] whereas he—he alone, independently of the work he does—ought to be treated as the effective subject of work and its true maker and creator. Precisely this reversal of order, whatever the program or name under which it occurs, should rightly be called "capitalism" —in the sense more fully explained below. Everybody knows that capitalism has a definite historical meaning as a system, an economic and social system, opposed to "socialism" or "communism." But in the light of the analysis of the fundamental reality of the whole economic process—first and

18

foremost of the production structure that work is—it should be recognized that the error of early capitalism can be repeated wherever man is in a way treated on the same level as the whole complex of the material means of production, as an instrument and not in accordance with the true dignity of his work—that is to say, where he is not treated as subject and maker, and for this very reason as the true purpose of the whole process of production.

This explains why the analysis of human work in the light of the words concerning man's "dominion" over the earth goes to the very heart of the ethical and social question. This concept should also find *a central place* in the whole *sphere of social and economic policy*, both within individual countries and in the wider field of international and intercontinental relationships, particularly with reference to the tensions making themselves felt in the world not only between East and West but also between North and South. Both John XXIII in the Encyclical *Mater et magistra* and Paul VI in the Encyclical *Populorum progressio* gave special attention to these dimensions of the modern ethical and social question.

8. Worker Solidarity

When dealing with human work in the fundamental dimension of its subject, that is to say, the human person doing the work, one must make at least a summary evaluation of developments during the ninety years since *Rerum novarum* in relation to the subjective dimension of work. Although the subject of work is always the same, that is to say man, nevertheless wide-ranging changes take place in the objective aspect. While one can say that, by reason of its subject, *work is one single thing* (one and unrepeatable every time), yet when one takes into consideration its objective directions one is forced to admit that *there exist many works*, many different sorts of work. The development of human civilization brings continual enrichment in this field. But at the same time, one cannot fail to note that in the process of this development not only do new forms of work appear but also others disappear. Even if one accepts that on the whole this is a normal phenomenon, it must still be seen whether certain ethically and socially dangerous irregularities creep in, and to what extent.

It was precisely one such *wide-ranging anomaly* that gave rise in the last century to what has been called "the worker question," sometimes described as "the proletariat question." This question and the problems connected with it gave rise to a just social reaction and caused the impetuous emergence of a great burst of solidarity between workers, first and foremost industrial workers. The call to solidarity and common action addressed to the workers—especially to those engaged in narrowly specialized, monotonous and depersonalized work in industrial plants, when the machine tends to dominate man —was important and eloquent from the point of view of social ethics. It was the reaction *against the degradation of man as the subject of work*, and against the unheard-of accompanying exploitation in the field of wages, working conditions and social security for the worker. This reaction united the working world in a community marked by great solidarity.

Following the lines laid down by the Encyclical *Rerum novarum* and many later documents of the Church's Magisterium, it must be frankly recognized that the reaction against the system of injustice and harm that cried to heaven for vengeance[13] and that weighed heavily upon workers in that period of rapid industrialization was justified *from the point of view of social morality*. This state of affairs was favored by the liberal sociopolitical system, which, in accordance with its "economistic" premises, strengthened and safeguarded economic initiative by the possessors of capital alone, but did not pay sufficient attention to the rights of the workers, on the grounds that human work is solely an instrument of production, and that capital is the basis, efficient factor and purpose of production.

From that time, worker solidarity, together with a clearer and more committed realization by others of workers' rights, has in many cases brought about profound changes. Various forms of neo-capitalism or collectivism have developed. Various new systems have been thought out. Workers can often share in running businesses and in controlling their productivity, and in fact do so. Through appropriate associations,

20

they exercise influence over conditions of work and pay, and also over social legislation. But at the same time various ideological or power systems, and new relationships which have arisen at various levels of society, *have allowed flagrant injustices to persist or have created new ones*. On the world level, the development of civilization and of communications has made possible a more complete diagnosis of the living and working conditions of man globally, but it has also revealed other forms of injustice, much more extensive than those which in the last century stimulated unity between workers for particular solidarity in the working world. This is true in countries which have completed a certain process of industrial revolution. It is also true in countries where the main working milieu continues to be *agriculture* or other similar occupations.

Movements of solidarity in the sphere of work—a solidarity that must never mean being closed to dialogue and collaboration with others—can be necessary also with reference to the condition of social groups that were not previously included in such movements but which, in changing social systems and conditions of living, are undergoing *what is in effect "proletarianization"* or which actually already find themselves in a "proletariat" situation, one which, even if not yet given that name, in fact deserves it. This can be true of certain categories or groups of the working "intelligentsia," especially when ever wider access to education and an ever increasing number of people with degrees or diplomas in the fields of their cultural preparation are accompanied by a drop in demand for their labor. This *unemployment of intellectuals* occurs or increases when the education available is not oriented towards the types of employment or service required by the true needs of society, or when there is less demand for work which requires education, at least professional education, than for manual labor, or when it is less well paid. Of course, education in itself is always valuable and an important enrichment of the human person; but in spite of that, "proletarianization" processes remain possible.

For this reason, *there must be continued study of the subject of work* and of the subject's living conditions. In order to achieve social justice in the various parts of the world, in the various countries, and in the relationships between them, there is a need for ever new *movements of solidarity of* the workers and *with* the workers. This solidarity must be present whenever it is called for by the social degrading of the subject of work, by exploitation of the workers, and by the growing areas of poverty and even hunger. The Church is firmly committed to this cause, for she considers it her mission, her service, a proof of her fidelity to Christ, so that she can truly be the "Church of the poor." And the "poor" appear under various forms; they appear in various places and at various times; in many cases they appear as a *result of the violation of the dignity of human work:* either because the opportunities for human work are limited as a result of the scourge of unemployment, or because a low value is put on work and the rights that flow from it, especially the right to a just wage and to the personal security of the worker and his or her family.

9. Work and Personal Dignity

Remaining within the context of man as the subject of work, it is now appropriate to touch upon, at least in a summary way, certain problems that *more closely define the dignity of human work,* in that they make it possible to characterize more fully its specific moral value. In doing this we must always keep in mind the biblical calling to "subdue the earth,"[14] in which is expressed the will of the Creator that work should enable man to achieve that "dominion" in the visible world that is proper to him.

God's fundamental and original intention with regard to man, whom He created in His image and after His likeness,[15] was not withdrawn or cancelled out even when man, having broken the original covenant with God, heard the words: "In the sweat of your face you shall eat bread."[16] These words refer to *the sometimes heavy toil* that from then onwards has accompanied human work; but they do not alter the fact that work is the means whereby man *achieves that "dominion"* which is proper to him over the visible world, by "subjecting" the earth. Toil is something that is universally known, for it is universally experienced. It is familiar to those doing physical work under sometimes exceptionally laborious conditions. It is familiar not only to agricultural workers, who spend long days working the land, which sometimes "bears thorns and thistles,"[17] but also to those who work in mines and quarries, to steelworkers at their blast-furnaces, to those who work in builders' yards and in construction work, often in danger of injury or death. It is likewise familiar to those at an intellectual workbench; to scientists; to those who bear the burden of grave responsibility for decisions that will have a vast impact on society. It is familiar to doctors and nurses, who spend days and nights at their patients' bedsides. It is familiar to women, who, sometimes without proper recognition on the part of society and even of their own families, bear the daily burden and responsibility for their homes and the upbringing of their children. *It is familiar to all workers*, and, since work is a universal calling, it is familiar to everyone.

And yet, in spite of all this toil—perhaps, in a sense, because of it—work is a good thing for man. Even though it bears the mark of a *bonum arduum*, in the terminology of St. Thomas,[18] this does not take away the fact that, as such, it is a good thing for man. It is not only good in the sense that it is useful or something to enjoy; it is also good as being something worthy, that is to say, something that corresponds to man's dignity, that expresses this dignity and increases it. If one wishes to define more clearly the ethical meaning of work, it is this truth that one must particularly keep in mind. Work is a good thing for man—a good thing for his humanity—because through work man *not only transforms nature*, adapting it to his own needs, but he also *achieves fulfillment* as a human being and indeed, in a sense, becomes "more a human being."

Without this consideration it is impossible to understand the meaning of the virtue of industriousness, and more particularly it is impossible to understand why industriousness should be a virtue: for virtue, as a moral habit, is something whereby man becomes good as man.[19] This fact in no way alters our justifiable anxiety that in work, whereby *matter* gains in *nobility*, *man* himself should not experience a *lowering* of his own dignity.[20] Again, it is well known that it is possible to use work in various ways *against man*, that it is possible to punish man with the system of forced labor in concentration

23

camps, that work can be made into a means for oppressing man, and that in various ways it is possible to exploit human labor, that is to say the worker. All this pleads in favor of the moral obligation to link industriousness as a virtue with *the social order of work*, which will enable man to become, in work, "more a human being" and not be degraded by it, not only because of the wearing out of his physical strength (which, at least up to a certain point, is inevitable), but especially through damage to the dignity and subjectivity that are proper to him.

10. Work and Society: Family and Nation

Having thus confirmed the personal dimension of human work, we must go on to the second *sphere of values* which is necessarily linked to work. Work constitutes a foundation for the formation of *family life*, which is a natural right and something that man is called to. These two spheres of values—one linked to work and the other consequent on the family nature of human life—must be properly united and must properly permeate each other. In a way, work is a condition for making it possible to found a family, since the family requires the means of subsistence which man normally gains through work. Work and industriousness also influence the whole *process of education* in the family, for the very reason that everyone "becomes a human being" through, among other things, work, and becoming a human being is precisely the main purpose of the whole process of education. Obviously, two aspects of work in a sense come into play here: the one making family life and its upkeep possible, and the other making possible the achievement of the purposes of the family, especially education. Nevertheless, these two aspects of work are linked to one another and are mutually complementary in various points.

It must be remembered and affirmed that the family constitutes one of the most important terms of reference for shaping the social and ethical order of human work. The teaching of the Church has always devoted special attention to this question, and in the present document we shall have to return to it. In fact, the family is simultaneously a *community made possible by work* and the first *school of work*, within the home, for every person.

The third sphere of values that emerges from this point of view—that of the subject of work—concerns the *great society* to which man belongs on the basis of particular cultural and historical links. This society—even when it has not yet taken on the mature form of a nation—is not only the great "educator" of every man, even though an indirect one (because each individual absorbs within the family the contents and values that go to make up the culture of a given nation); it is also a great historical and social incarnation of the work of all generations. All of this brings it about that man combines his deepest human identity with membership of a nation, and intends his work also to increase the common good developed together with his compatriots, thus realizing that in this way work serves to add to the heritage of the whole human family, of all the people living in the world.

These three spheres are always *important for human work* in its subjective dimension. And this dimension, that is to say, the concrete reality of the worker, takes precedence over the objective dimension. In the subjective dimension there is realized, first of all, that "dominion" over the world of nature to which man is called from the beginning according to the words of the book of Genesis. The very process of "subduing the earth," that is to say work, is marked in the course of history, and especially in recent centuries, by an immense development of technological means. This is an advantageous and positive phenomenon, on condition that the objective dimension of work does not gain the upper hand over the subjective dimension, depriving man of his dignity and inalienable rights or reducing them.

III
CONFLICT BETWEEN LABOR
AND CAPITAL
IN THE PRESENT PHASE OF HISTORY

11. Dimensions of the Conflict

The sketch of the basic problems of work outlined above draws inspiration from the texts at the beginning of the Bible and in a sense forms the very framework of the Church's teaching, which has remained unchanged throughout the centuries within the context of different historical experiences. However, the experiences preceding and following the publication of the Encyclical *Rerum novarum* form a background that endows that teaching with particular expressiveness and the eloquence of living relevance. In this analysis, work is seen as a great reality with a fundamental influence on the shaping in a human way of the world that the Creator has entrusted to man; it is a reality closely linked with man as the subject of work and with man's rational activity. In the normal course of events this reality fills human life and strongly affects its value and meaning. Even when it is accompanied by toil and effort, work is still something good, and so man develops through love for work. This entirely *positive and creative, educational and meritorious character of man's work* must be the basis for the judgments and decisions being made today in its regard in spheres that include *human rights*, as is evidenced by the international *declarations* on work and the many *labor codes* prepared either by the competent legislative institutions in the various countries or by organizations devoting their social, or scientific and social, activity to the problems of work. One organization fostering such initiatives on the international level is the International Labor Organization, the oldest specialized agency of the United Nations Organization.

In the following part of these considerations I intend to return in greater detail to these important questions, recalling at least the basic elements of the Church's teaching on the matter. I must however first touch on a very important field of questions in which her teaching has taken shape in this latest period, the one marked and in a sense symbolized by the publication of the Encyclical *Rerum novarum.*

Throughout this period, which is by no means yet over, the issue of work has of course been posed on the basis of the great *conflict* that in the age of, and together with, industrial development emerged *between "capital" and "labor,"* that is to say between the small but highly influential group of entrepreneurs, owners or holders of the means of production, and the broader multitude of people who lacked these means and who shared in the process of production solely by their labor. The conflict originated in the fact that the workers put their powers at the disposal of the entrepreneurs, and these, following the principle of maximum profit, tried to establish the lowest possible wages for the work done by the employees. In addition there were other elements of exploitation, connected with the lack of safety at work and of safeguards regarding the health and living conditions of the workers and their families.

This conflict, interpreted by some as a socioeconomic *class conflict*, found expression in the *ideological conflict* between liberalism, understood as the ideology of capitalism, and Marxism, understood as the ideology of scientific socialism and communism, which professes to act as the spokesman for the working class and the worldwide proletariat. Thus the real conflict between labor and capital was transformed into *a systematic class struggle*, conducted not only by ideological means but also and chiefly by political means. We are familiar with the history of this conflict and with the demands of both sides. The Marxist program, based on the philosophy of Marx and Engels, sees in class struggle the only way to eliminate class injustices in society and to eliminate the classes themselves. Putting this program into practice presupposes *the collectivization of the means of production* so that, through the transfer of these means from private hands to the collectivity, human labor will be preserved from exploitation.

This is the goal of the struggle carried on by political as well as ideological means. In accordance with the principle of "the dictatorship of the proletariat," the groups that as political parties follow the guidance of Marxist ideology aim, by the use of various kinds of influence, including revolutionary pressure, to win *a monopoly of power in each society*, in order to introduce the collectivist system into it by eliminating private ownership of the means of production. According to the principal ideologists and leaders of this broad international movement, the purpose of this program of action is to achieve the social revolution and to introduce socialism and, finally, the communist system throughout the world.

As we touch on this extremely important field of issues, which constitute not only a theory but a whole fabric of socio-economic, political, and international life in our age, we cannot *go into the details*, nor is this necessary, for they are known both from the vast literature on the subject and by experience. Instead, we must leave the context of these issues and go back to the fundamental issue of human work, which is the main subject of the considerations in this document. It is clear, indeed, that this issue, which is of such importance for man— it constitutes one of the fundamental dimensions of his earthly existence and of his vocation—can also be explained only by taking into account the full context of the contemporary situation.

12. The Priority of Labor

The structure of the present-day situation is deeply marked by many conflicts caused by man, and the technological means produced by human work play a primary role in it. We should also consider here the prospect of worldwide catastrophe in the case of a nuclear war, which would have almost unimaginable possibilities of destruction. In view of this situation we must first of all recall a principle that has always been taught by the Church: *the principle of the priority of labor over capital*. This principle directly concerns the process of production: in this process labor is always a primary *efficient cause*, while capital, the whole collection of

28

means of production, remains a mere *instrument* or instrumental cause. This principle is an evident truth that emerges from the whole of man's historical experience.

When we read in the first chapter of the Bible that man is to subdue the earth, we know that these words refer to all the resources contained in the visible world and placed at man's disposal. However, these resources *can serve man only through work*. From the beginning there is also linked with work the question of ownership, for the only means that man has for causing the resources hidden in nature to serve himself and others is his work. And to be able through his work to make these resources bear fruit, man takes over ownership of small parts of the various riches of nature: those beneath the ground, those in the sea, on land, or in space. He takes all these things over by making them his workbench. He takes them over through work and for work.

The same principle applies in the successive phases of this process, in which *the first phase* always remains the relationship of man with *the resources and riches of nature*. The whole of the effort to acquire knowledge with the aim of discovering these riches and specifying the various ways in which they can be used by man and for man teaches us that everything that comes from man throughout the whole process of economic production, whether labor or the whole collection of means of production and the technology connected with these means (meaning the capability to use them in work), presupposes these riches and resources of the visible world, riches and resources *that man finds* and does not create. In a sense man finds them already prepared, ready for him to discover them and to use them correctly in the productive process. In every phase of the development of his work, man comes up against the leading role of *the gift made* by "nature," that is to say, in the final analysis, *by the Creator*. At the beginning of man's work is the mystery of creation. This affirmation, already indicated as my starting point, is the guiding thread of this document, and will be further developed in the last part of these reflections.

Further consideration of this question should confirm our conviction of *the priority of human labor over* what in the

29

course of time we have grown accustomed to calling *capital*. Since the concept of capital includes not only the natural resources placed at man's disposal but also the whole collection of means by which man appropriates natural resources and transforms them in accordance with his needs (and thus in a sense humanizes them), it must immediately be noted that *all these means are the result of the historical heritage of human labor*. All the means of production, from the most primitive to the ultramodern ones—it is man that has gradually developed them: man's experience and intellect. In this way there have appeared not only the simplest instruments for cultivating the earth but also, through adequate progress in science and technology, the more modern and complex ones: machines, factories, laboratories, and computers. Thus *everything that is at the service of work*, everything that in the present state of technology constitutes its ever more highly perfected "instrument," *is the result of work*.

This gigantic and powerful instrument—the whole collection of means of production that in a sense are considered synonymous with "capital"—is the result of work and bears the signs of human labor. At the present stage of technological advance, when man, who is the subject of work, wishes to make use of this collection of modern instruments, the means of production, he must first assimilate cognitively the result of the work of the people who invented those instruments, who planned them, built them and perfected them, and who continue to do so. *Capacity for work*—that is to say, for sharing efficiently in the modern production process—demands greater and greater *preparation* and, before all else, proper *training*. Obviously, it remains clear that every human being sharing in the production process, even if he or she is only doing the kind of work for which no special training or qualifications are required, is the real efficient subject in this production process, while the whole collection of instruments, no matter how perfect they may be in themselves, is only a mere instrument subordinate to human labor.

This truth, which is part of the abiding heritage of the Church's teaching, must always be emphasized with reference to the question of the labor system and with regard to the

30

whole socioeconomic system. We must emphasize and give prominence to the primacy of man in the production process, *the primacy of man over things*. Everything contained in the concept of capital in the strict sense is only a collection of things. Man, as the subject of work, and independently of the work that he does—man alone is a person. This truth has important and decisive consequences.

13. Economism and Materialism

In the light of the above truth we see clearly, first of all, that capital cannot be separated from labor; in no way can labor be opposed to capital or capital to labor, and still less can the actual people behind these concepts be opposed to each other, as will be explained later. A labor system can be right, in the sense of being in conformity with the very essence of the issue, and in the sense of being intrinsically true and also morally legitimate, if in its very basis *it overcomes the opposition between labor and capital* through an effort at being shaped in accordance with the principle put forward above: the principle of the substantial and real priority of labor, of the subjectivity of human labor and its effective participation in the whole production process, independently of the nature of the services provided by the worker.

Opposition between labor and capital does not spring from the structure of the production process or from the structure of the economic process. In general the latter process demonstrates that labor and what we are accustomed to call capital are intermingled; it shows that they are inseparably linked. Working at any workbench, whether a relatively primitive or an ultramodern one, a man can easily see that *through his work he enters into two inheritances:* the inheritance of what is given to the whole of humanity in the resources of nature, and the inheritance of what others have already developed on the basis of those resources, primarily by developing technology, that is to say, by producing a whole collection of increasingly perfect instruments for work. In working, man also "enters into the labor of others."[21] Guided

31

both by our intelligence and by the faith that draws light from the word of God, we have no difficulty in accepting this image of the sphere and process of man's labor. It is *a consistent image, one that is humanistic as well as theological*. In it man is the master of the creatures placed at his disposal in the visible world. If some dependence is discovered in the work process, it is dependence on the Giver of all the resources of creation, and also on other human beings, those to whose work and initiative we owe the perfected and increased possibilities of our own work. All that we can say of everything in the production process which constitutes a whole collection of "things," the instruments, the capital, is that it *conditions* man's work; we cannot assert that it constitutes as it were an impersonal "subject" *putting* man and man's work *into a position of dependence*.

This *consistent image*, in which the principle of the primacy of person over things is strictly preserved, *was broken up in human thought*, sometimes after a long period of incubation in practical living. The break occurred in such a way that labor was separated from capital and set in opposition to it, and capital was set in opposition to labor, as though they were two impersonal forces, two production factors juxtaposed in the same "economistic" perspective. This way of stating the issue contained a fundamental error, what we can call *the error of economism*, that of considering human labor solely according to its economic purpose. This fundamental error of thought can and must be called *an error of materialism*, in that economism directly or indirectly includes a conviction of the primacy and superiority of the material, and directly or indirectly places the spiritual and the personal (man's activity, moral values and such matters) in a position of subordination to material reality. This is still not *theoretical materialism* in the full sense of the term, but it is certainly *practical materialism*, a materialism judged capable of satisfying man's needs, not so much on the grounds of premises derived from materialist theory, as on the grounds of a particular way of evaluating things, and so on the grounds of a certain hierarchy of goods based on the greater immediate attractiveness of what is material.

The error of thinking in the categories of economism went hand in hand with the formation of a materialist philosophy, as this philosophy developed from the most elementary and common phase (also called common materialism, because it professes to reduce spiritual reality to a superfluous phenomenon) to the phase of what is called dialectical materialism. However, within the framework of the present consideration, it seems that *economism had a decisive importance* for the fundamental issue of human work, in particular for the separation of labor and capital and for setting them up in opposition as two production factors viewed in the above-mentioned economistic perspective; and it seems that economism influenced this non-humanistic way of stating the issue before the materialist philosophical system did. Nevertheless it is obvious that materialism, including its dialectical form, is incapable of providing sufficient and definitive bases for thinking about human work, in order that the primacy of man over the capital instrument, the primacy of the person over things, may find in it adequate and irrefutable *confirmation and support.* In dialectical materialism too man is not first and foremost the subject of work and the efficient cause of the production process, but continues to be understood and treated, in dependence on what is material, as a kind of "resultant" of the economic or production relations prevailing at a given period.

Obviously, the antinomy between labor and capital under consideration here—*the antinomy* in which *labor was separated from capital and set up in opposition to it,* in a certain sense on the ontic level, as if it were just an element like any other in the economic process—did not originate merely in the philosophy and economic theories of the eighteenth century; rather it originated in the whole of the *economic and social practice* of that time, the time of the birth and rapid development of industrialization, in which what was mainly seen was the possibility of vastly increasing material wealth, means, while the end, that is to say, man, who should be served by the means, was ignored. It was this practical error that *struck a blow* first and foremost against human labor, against *the working man,* and caused the ethically just social reaction already spoken of above. The same error, which is now part of

33

history, and which was connected with the period of primitive capitalism and liberalism, can nevertheless be repeated in other circumstances of time and place, if people's thinking starts from the same theoretical or practical premises. The only chance there seems to be for radically overcoming this error is through adequate changes both in theory and in practice, changes *in line with* the definite *conviction of the primacy* of the person over things, and of human *labor over capital* as a whole collection of means of production.

14. Work and Ownership

The historical process briefly presented here has certainly gone beyond its initial phase, but it is still taking place and indeed is spreading in the relationships between nations and continents. It needs to be specified further from another point of view. It is obvious that, when we speak of opposition between labor and capital, we are not dealing only with abstract concepts or "impersonal forces" operating in economic production. Behind both concepts there are people, living, actual people: on the one side are those who do the work without being the owners of the means of production, and on the other side those who act as entrepreneurs and who own these means or represent the owners. Thus *the issue of ownership or property* enters from the beginning into the whole of this difficult historical process. The Encyclical *Rerum novarum*, which has the social question as its theme, stresses this issue also, recalling and confirming the Church's teaching on ownership, on the right to private property even when it is a question of the means of production. The Encyclical *Mater et magistra* did the same.

The above principle, as it was then stated and as it is still taught by the Church, *diverges* radically from the program of *collectivism* as proclaimed by Marxism and put into practice in various countries in the decades following the time of Leo XIII's encyclical. At the same time it differs from the program of *capitalism* practiced by liberalism and by the political systems inspired by it. In the latter case, the difference consists in the way the right to ownership or property is understood.

34

Christian tradition has never upheld this right as absolute and untouchable. On the contrary, it has always understood this right within the broader context of the right common to all to use the goods of the whole of creation: *the right to private property is subordinated to the right to common use*, to the fact that goods are meant for everyone.

Furthermore, in the Church's teaching, ownership has never been understood in a way that could constitute grounds for social conflict in labor. As mentioned above, property is acquired first of all through work in order that it may serve work. This concerns in a special way ownership of the means of production. Isolating these means as a separate property in order to set it up in the form of "capital" in opposition to "labor"—and even to practice exploitation of labor—is contrary to the very nature of these means and their possession. They cannot be *possessed against labor*, they cannot even be *possessed for possession's sake*, because the only legitimate title to their possession—whether in the form of private ownership or in the form of public or collective ownership—is *that they should serve labor*, and thus, by serving labor, that they should make possible the achievement of the first principle of this order, namely, the universal destination of goods and the right to common use of them. From this point of view, therefore, in consideration of human labor and of common access to the goods meant for man, one cannot exclude the *socialization*, in suitable conditions, of certain means of production. In the course of the decades since the publication of the Encyclical *Rerum novarum*, the Church's teaching has always recalled all these principles, going back to the arguments formulated in a much older tradition, for example, the well-known arguments of the *Summa Theologiae* of St. Thomas Aquinas.[22]

In the present document, which has human work as its main theme, it is right to confirm all the effort with which the Church's teaching has striven and continues to strive always to ensure the priority of work and, thereby, man's character as a *subject* in social life and, especially, in the dynamic *structure of the whole economic process*. From this point of view the position of "rigid" capitalism continues to remain unacceptable, namely the position that defends the exclusive right to

35

private ownership of the means of production as an untouchable "dogma" of economic life. The principle of respect for work demands that this right should undergo a constructive revision, both in theory and in practice. If it is true that capital, as the whole of the means of production, is at the same time the product of the work of generations, it is equally true that capital is being unceasingly created through the work done with the help of all these means of production, and these means can be seen as a great workbench at which the present generation of workers is working day after day. Obviously we are dealing here with different kinds of work, not only so-called manual labor but also the many forms of intellectual work, including white-collar work and management.

In the light of the above, the many proposals put forward by experts in Catholic social teaching and by the highest Magisterium of the Church take on special significance:[23] *proposals* for *joint ownership of the means of work*, sharing by the workers in the management and/or profits of business, so-called shareholding by labor, etc. Whether these various proposals can or cannot be applied concretely, it is clear that recognition of the proper position of labor and the worker in the production process demands various adaptations in the sphere of the right to ownership of the means of production. This is so not only in view of older situations but also, first and foremost, in view of the whole of the situation and the problems in the second half of the present century with regard to the so-called Third World and the various new independent countries that have arisen, especially in Africa but elsewhere as well, in place of the colonial territories of the past.

Therefore, while the position of "rigid" capitalism must undergo continual revision, in order to be reformed from the point of view of human rights, both human rights in the widest sense and those linked with man's work, it must be stated that, from the same point of view, these many deeply desired reforms cannot be achieved by an *a priori elimination of private ownership of the means of production.* For it must be noted that merely taking these means of production (capital) out of the hands of their private owners is not enough to ensure their satisfactory socialization. They cease to be the property of a certain social group, namely the private owners, and become the property of organized society, coming under the administration and direct control of another group of people, namely those who, though not owning them, from the fact of exercising power in society *manage* them on the level of the whole national or the local economy.

This group in authority may carry out its task satisfactorily from the point of view of the priority of labor; but it may also carry it out badly by claiming for itself *a monopoly of the administration and disposal* of the means of production and not refraining even from offending basic human rights. Thus, merely converting the means of production into State property in the collectivist system is by no means equivalent to "socializing" that property. We can speak of socializing only when the subject character of society is ensured, that is to say, when on the basis of his work each person is fully entitled to consider himself a part-owner of the great workbench at which he is working with every one else. A way towards that goal could be found by associating labor with the ownership of capital, as far as possible, and by producing a wide range of intermediate bodies with economic, social and cultural purposes; they would be bodies enjoying real autonomy with regard to the public powers, pursuing their specific aims in honest collaboration with each other and in subordination to the demands of the common good, and they would be living communities both in form and in substance, in the sense that the members of each body would be looked upon and treated as persons and encouraged to take an active part in the life of the body.[24]

15. The "Personalist" Argument

Thus, *the principle of the priority of labor* over capital is a postulate of the order of social morality. It has key importance both in the system built on the principle of private ownership of the means of production and also in the system in which private ownership of these means has been limited even in a radical way. Labor is in a sense inseparable from capital; in no way does it accept the antinomy, that is to say, the separation

37

and opposition with regard to the means of production that has weighed upon human life in recent centuries as a result of merely economic premises. When man works, using all the means of production, he also wishes the fruit of this work to be used by himself and others, and he wishes to be able to take part in the very work process as a sharer in responsibility and creativity at the workbench to which he applies himself.

From this spring certain specific rights of workers, corresponding to the obligation of work. They will be discussed later. But here it must be emphasized, in general terms, that the person who works desires *not only* due *remuneration* for his work; he also wishes that, within the production process, provision be made for him to be able to *know* that in his work, even on something that is owned in common, he is working *"for himself."* This awareness is extinguished within him in a system of excessive bureaucratic centralization, which makes the worker feel that he is just a cog in a huge machine moved from above, that he is for more reasons than one a mere production instrument rather than a true subject of work with an initiative of his own. The Church's teaching has always expressed the strong and deep conviction that man's work concerns not only the economy but also, and especially, personal values. The economic system itself and the production process benefit precisely when these personal values are fully respected. In the mind of St. Thomas Aquinas,[25] this is the principal reason in favor of private ownership of the means of production. While we accept that for certain well-founded reasons exceptions can be made to the principle of private ownership—in our own time we even see that the system of "socialized ownership" has been introduced—nevertheless the personalist *argument still holds good* both on the level of principles and *on the practical level.* If it is to be rational and fruitful, any socialization of the means of production must take this argument into consideration. Every effort must be made to ensure that in this kind of system also the human person can preserve his awareness of working "for himself." If this is not done, incalculable damage is inevitably done throughout the economic process, not only economic damage but first and foremost damage to man.

IV
RIGHTS OF WORKERS

16. Within the Broad Context of Human Rights

While work, in all its many senses, is an obligation, that is to say a duty, it is also a source of rights on the part of the *worker*. These rights must be examined in the broad *context of human rights as a whole*, which are connatural with man, and many of which are proclaimed by various international organizations and increasingly guaranteed by the individual States for their citizens. Respect for this broad range of human rights constitutes the fundamental condition for peace in the modern world: peace both within individual countries and societies and in international relations, as the Church's Magisterium has several times noted, especially since the Encyclical *Pacem in terris*. The *human rights that flow from work* are part of the broader context of those fundamental rights of the person.

However, within this context they have a specific character corresponding to the specific nature of human work as outlined above. It is in keeping with this character that we must view them. Work is, as has been said, *an obligation*, that is to say, *a duty*, *on the part of man*. This is true *in all the many meanings of the word*. Man must work, both because the Creator has commanded it and because of his own humanity, which requires work in order to be maintained and developed. Man must work out of regard for others, especially his own family, but also for the society he belongs to, the country of which he is a child, and the whole human family of which he is a member, since he is the heir to the work of generations and at the same time a sharer in building the future of those who will come after him in the succession of history. All this constitutes the moral obligation of work, understood in its wide sense. When we have to consider the moral rights, corresponding to this obligation, of every person with regard to work, we must always keep before our eyes the whole vast range of points of reference in which the labor of every working subject is manifested.

For when we speak of the obligation of work and of the rights of the worker that correspond to this obligation, we think in the first place of the relationship between *the employer, direct or indirect, and the worker*.

The distinction between the direct and the indirect employer is seen to be very important when one considers both the way in which labor is actually organized and the possibility of the formation of just or unjust relationships in the field of labor.

Since *the direct employer* is the person or institution with whom the worker enters directly into a work contract in accordance with definite conditions, we must understand as *the indirect* employer many different factors, other than the direct employer, that exercise a determining influence on the shaping both of the work contract and, consequently, of just or unjust relationships in the field of human labor.

17. Direct and Indirect Employer

The concept of indirect employer includes both persons and institutions of various kinds, and also collective labor contracts and the *principles* of conduct which are laid down by these persons and institutions and which determine the whole socioeconomic *system* or are its result. The concept of "indirect employer" thus refers to many different elements. The responsibility of the indirect employer differs from that of the direct employer—the term itself indicates that the responsibility is less direct—but it remains a true responsibility: the indirect employer substantially determines one or other facet of the labor relationship, thus conditioning the conduct of the direct employer when the latter determines in concrete terms the actual work contract and labor relations. This is not to absolve the direct employer from his own responsibility, but only to draw attention to the whole network of influences that condition his conduct. When it is a question of establishing *an ethically correct labor policy*, all these influences must be kept in mind. A policy is correct when the objective rights of the worker are fully respected.

The concept of indirect employer is applicable to every society, and in the first place to the State. For it is the State that must conduct a just labor policy. However, it is common knowledge that in the present system of economic relations in the world there are numerous *links between* individual *States*, links that find expression, for instance, in the import and export process, that is to say, in the mutual exchange of economic goods, whether raw materials, semi-manufactured goods, or finished industrial products. These links also create mutual *dependence*, and as a result it would be difficult to speak, in the case of any State, even the economically most powerful, of complete self-sufficiency or autarky.

Such a system of mutual dependence is in itself normal. However, it can easily become an occasion for various forms of exploitation or injustice and as a result influence the labor policy of individual States; and finally it can influence the individual worker, who is the proper subject of labor. For instance the *highly industrialized countries*, and even more the businesses that direct on a large scale the means of industrial production (the companies referred to as multinational or transnational), fix the highest possible prices for their products, while trying at the same time to fix the lowest possible prices for raw materials or semi-manufactured goods. This is one of the causes of an ever-increasing disproportion between national incomes. The gap between most of the richest countries and the poorest ones is not diminishing or being stabilized but is increasing more and more, to the detriment, obviously, of the poor countries. Evidently this must have an effect on local labor policy and on the worker's situation in the economically disadvantaged societies. Finding himself in a system thus conditioned, the direct employer fixes working conditions below the objective requirements of the workers, especially if he himself wishes to obtain the highest possible profits from the business which he runs (or from the businesses which he runs, in the case of a situation of "socialized" ownership of the means of production).

41

It is easy to see that this framework of forms of dependence linked with the concept of the indirect employer is enormously extensive and complicated. It is determined, in a sense, by *all* the elements that are decisive for economic life *within a given society and State*, but also by much wider links and forms of dependence. The attainment of the worker's rights cannot however be doomed to be merely a result of economic systems which on a larger or smaller scale are guided chiefly by the criterion of maximum profit. On the contrary, it is respect for the objective rights of the worker—every kind of worker: manual or intellectual, industrial or agricultural, etc. —that must constitute *the adequate and fundamental criterion* for shaping the whole economy, both on the level of the individual society and State and within the whole of the world economic policy and of the systems of international relationships that derive from it.

Influence in this direction should be exercised by all *the International Organizations* whose concern it is, beginning with the United Nations Organization. It appears that the International Labor Organization and the Food and Agriculture Organization of the United Nations and other bodies too have fresh contributions to offer on this point in particular. Within the individual States there are ministries or *public departments* and also various *social institutions* set up for this purpose. All of this effectively indicates the importance of the indirect employer—as has been said above—in achieving full respect for the worker's rights, since the rights of the human person are the key element in the whole of the social moral order.

18. The Employment Issue

When we consider the rights of workers in relation to the "indirect employer," that is to say, all the agents at the national and international level that are responsible for the whole orientation of labor policy, we must first direct our attention to *a fundamental issue:* the question of finding work, or, in other words, the issue of *suitable employment for all who are capable of it.* The opposite of a just and right situation in this field is unemployment, that is to say the lack of work for those who are capable of it. It can be a question of general unemployment or of unemployment in certain sectors of work. The role of the agents included under the title of indirect employer is *to act against unemployment*, which in all cases is an evil, and which, when it reaches a certain level, can become a real social disaster. It is particularly painful when it especially affects young people, who after appropriate cultural, technical and professional preparation fail to find work, and see their sincere wish to work and their readiness to take on their own responsibility for the economic and social development of the community sadly frustrated. The obligation to provide unemployment benefits, that is to say, the duty to make suitable grants indispensable for the subsistence of unemployed workers and their families, is a duty springing from the fundamental principle of the moral order in this sphere, namely the principle of the common use of goods or, to put it in another and still simpler way, the right to life and subsistence.

In order to meet the danger of unemployment and to ensure employment for all, the agents defined here as "indirect employer" must make provision for *overall planning* with regard to the different kinds of work by which not only the economic life but also the cultural life of a given society is shaped; they must also give attention to organizing that work in a correct and rational way. In the final analysis this overall concern weighs on the shoulders of the State, but it cannot mean one-sided centralization by the public authorities. Instead, what is in question is a just and rational *coordination*, within the framework of which the *initiative* of individuals, free groups and local work centers and complexes must be *safeguarded*, keeping in mind what has been said above with regard to the subject character of human labor.

The fact of the mutual dependence of societies and States and the need to collaborate in various areas mean that, while preserving the sovereign rights of each society and State in the field of planning and organizing labor in its own society, action in this important area must also be taken in the dimension of *international collaboration* by means of the necessary

43

treaties and agreements. Here too the criterion for these pacts and agreements must more and more be the criterion of human work considered as a fundamental right of all human beings, work which gives similar rights to all those who work, in such a way that the living standard of the workers in the different societies will *less and less show those disturbing differences* which are unjust and are apt to provoke even violent reactions. The International Organizations have an enormous part to play in this area. They must let themselves be guided by an exact diagnosis of the complex situations and of the influence exercised by natural, historical, civil and other such circumstances. They must also be more highly operative with regard to plans for action jointly decided on, that is to say, they must be more effective in carrying them out.

In this direction it is possible to actuate a plan for universal and proportionate progress by all, in accordance with the guidelines of Paul VI's Encyclical *Populorum progressio*. It must be stressed that the constitutive element in this *progress* and also the most adequate *way to verify it* in a spirit of justice and peace, which the Church proclaims and for which she does not cease to pray to the Father of all individuals and of all peoples, is *the continual reappraisal of man's work*, both in the aspect of its objective finality and in the aspect of the dignity of the subject of all work, that is to say, man. The progress in question must be made through man and for man and it must produce its fruit in man. A test of this progress will be the increasingly mature recognition of the purpose of work and increasingly universal respect for the rights inherent in work in conformity with the dignity of man, the subject of work.

Rational planning and the proper organization of human labor in keeping with individual societies and States should also facilitate the discovery of the right proportions between the different kinds of employment: work on the land, in industry, in the various services, white-collar work and scientific or artistic work, in accordance with the capacities of individuals and for the common good of each society and of the whole of mankind. The organization of human life in accordance with the many possibilities of labor should be matched by a suitable *system of instruction* and education, aimed first of all at
44

developing mature human beings, but also aimed at preparing people specifically for assuming to good advantage an appropriate place in the vast and socially differentiated world of work.

As we view the whole human family throughout the world, we cannot fail to be struck by *a disconcerting fact* of immense proportions: the fact that, while conspicuous natural resources remain unused, there are huge numbers of people who are unemployed or under-employed and countless multitudes of people suffering from hunger. This is a fact that without any doubt demonstrates that both within the individual political communities and in their relationships on the continental and world level there is something wrong with the organization of work and employment, precisely at the most critical and socially most important points.

19. Wages and Other Social Benefits

After outlining the important role that concern for providing employment for all workers plays in safeguarding respect for the inalienable rights of man in view of his work, it is worthwhile taking a closer look at these rights, which in the final analysis are formed within the relationship *between worker and direct employer*. All that has been said above on the subject of the indirect employer is aimed at defining these relationships more exactly, by showing the many forms of conditioning within which these relationships are indirectly formed. This consideration does not however have a purely descriptive purpose; it is not a brief treatise on economics or politics. It is a matter of highlighting the *deontological and moral aspect*. The key problem of social ethics in this case is that of *just remuneration* for work done. In the context of the present there is no more important way for securing a just relationship between the worker and the employer than that constituted by remuneration for work. Whether the work is done in a system of private ownership of the means of production or in a system where ownership has undergone a certain "socialization," the relationship between the employer (first

45

and foremost the direct employer) and the worker is resolved on the basis of the wage, that is, through just remuneration for work done.

It should also be noted that the justice of a socioeconomic system and, in each case, its just functioning, deserve in the final analysis to be evaluated by the way in which man's work is properly remunerated in the system. Here we return once more to the first principle of the whole ethical and social order, namely, *the principle of the common use of goods.* In every system, regardless of the fundamental relationships within it between capital and labor, wages, that is to say *remuneration for work*, are still a *practical means* whereby the vast majority of people can have access to those goods which are intended for common use: both the goods of nature and manufactured goods. Both kinds of goods become accessible to the worker through the wage which he receives as remuneration for his work. Hence, in every case, a just wage is the concrete means of *verifying the justice* of the whole socioeconomic system and, in any case, of checking that it is functioning justly. It is not the only means of checking, but it is a particularly important one and, in a sense, the key means.

This means of checking concerns above all the family. Just remuneration for the work of an adult who is responsible for a family means remuneration which will suffice for establishing and properly maintaining a family and for providing security for its future. Such remuneration can be given either through what is called a *family wage*—that is, a single salary given to the head of the family for his work, sufficient for the needs of the family without the other spouse having to take up gainful employment outside the home—or through *other social measures* such as family allowances or grants to mothers devoting themselves exclusively to their families. These grants should correspond to the actual needs, that is, to the number of dependents for as long as they are not in a position to assume proper responsibility for their own lives.

Experience confirms that there must be *a social re-evaluation of the mother's role*, of the toil connected with it, and of the need that children have for care, love and affection in order that they may develop into responsible, morally and
46

religiously mature and psychologically stable persons. It will redound to the credit of society to make it possible for a mother—without inhibiting her freedom, without psychological or practical discrimination, and without penalizing her as compared with other women—to devote herself to taking care of her children and educating them in accordance with their needs, which vary with age. Having to abandon these tasks in order to take up paid work outside the home is wrong from the point of view of the good of society and of the family when it contradicts or hinders these primary goals of the mission of a mother.[26]

In this context it should be emphasized that, on a more general level, the whole labor process must be organized and adapted in such a way as to respect the requirements of the person and his or her forms of life, above all life in the home, taking into account the individual's age and sex. It is a fact that in many societies women work in nearly every sector of life. But it is fitting that they should be able to fulfill their tasks *in accordance with their own nature*, without being discriminated against and without being excluded from jobs for which they are capable, but also without lack of respect for their family aspirations and for their specific role in contributing, together with men, to the good of society. The *true advancement of women* requires that labor should be structured in such a way that women do not have to pay for their advancement by abandoning what is specific to them and at the expense of the family, in which women as mothers have an irreplaceable role.

Besides wages, various *social benefits* intended to ensure the life and health of workers and their families play a part here. The expenses involved in health care, especially in the case of accidents at work, demand that medical assistance should be easily available for workers, and that as far as possible it should be cheap or even free of charge. Another sector regarding benefits is the sector associated with the *right to rest*. In the first place this involves a regular weekly rest comprising at least Sunday, and also a longer period of rest, namely the holiday or vacation taken once a year or possibly in several shorter periods during the year. A third sector concerns the

47

right to a pension and to insurance for old age and in case of accidents at work. Within the sphere of these principal rights, there develops a whole system of particular rights which, together with remuneration for work, determine the correct relationship between worker and employer. Among these rights there should never be overlooked the right to a working environment and to manufacturing processes which are not harmful to the workers' physical health or to their moral integrity.

20. Importance of Unions

All these rights, together with the need for the workers themselves to secure them, give rise to yet another right: *the right of association*, that is to form associations for the purpose of defending the vital interests of those employed in the various professions. These associations are called *labor or trade unions*. The vital interests of the workers are to a certain extent common for all of them; at the same time however each type of work, each profession, has its own specific character which should find a particular reflection in these organizations.

In a sense, unions go back to the medieval guilds of artisans, insofar as those organizations brought together people belonging to the same craft and thus *on the basis of their work*. However, unions differ from the guilds on this essential point: the modern unions grew up from the struggle of the workers— workers in general but especially the industrial workers—to protect their *just rights* vis-a-vis the entrepreneurs and the owners of the means of production. Their task is to defend the existential interests of workers in all sectors in which their rights are concerned. The experience of history teaches that organizations of this type are an indispensable *element of social life*, especially in modern industrialized societies. Obviously, this does not mean that only industrial workers can set up associations of this type. Representatives of every profession can use them to ensure their own rights. Thus there are unions of agricultural workers and of white-collar workers; there are also employers' associations. All, as has been said above, are further divided into groups or subgroups according to particular professional specializations.

48

Catholic social teaching does not hold that unions are no more than a reflection of the "class" structure of society and that they are a mouthpiece for a class struggle which inevitably governs social life. They are indeed *a mouthpiece for the struggle for social justice*, for the just rights of working people in accordance with their individual professions. However, this struggle should be seen as a normal endeavor "for" the just good: in the present case, for the good which corresponds to the needs and merits of working people associated by profession; but it *is not a struggle "against" others*. Even if in controversial questions the struggle takes on a character of opposition towards others, this is because it aims at the good of social justice, not for the sake of "struggle" or in order to eliminate the opponent. It is characteristic of work that it first and foremost unites people. In this consists its social power: the power to build a community. In the final analysis, both those who work and those who manage the means of production or who own them must in some way be united in this community. *In the light of this fundamental structure* of all work—in the light of the fact that, in the final analysis, labor and capital are indispensable components of the process of production in any social system—it is clear that, even if it is because of their work needs that people unite to secure their rights, their union remains a constructive factor of *social order* and *solidarity*, and it is impossible to ignore it.

Just efforts to secure the rights of workers who are united by the same profession should always take into account the limitations imposed by the general economic situation of the country. Union demands cannot be turned into a kind of *group or class "egoism,"* although they can and should also aim at correcting—with a view to the common good of the whole of society—everything defective in the system of ownership of the means of production or in the way these are managed. Social and socioeconomic life is certainly like a system of "connected vessels," and every social activity directed towards safeguarding the rights of particular groups should adapt itself to this system.

In this sense, union activity undoubtedly enters the field of *politics*, understood as *prudent concern for the common*

49

good. However, the role of unions is not to "play politics" in the sense that the expression is commonly understood today. Unions do not have the character of political parties struggling for power; they should not be subjected to the decision of political parties or have too close links with them. In fact, in such a situation they easily lose contact with their specific role, which is to secure the just rights of workers within the framework of the common good of the whole of society; instead they become *an instrument used for other purposes*.

Speaking of the protection of the just rights of workers according to their individual professions, we must of course always keep in mind that which determines the subjective character of work in each profession, but at the same time, indeed before all else, we must keep in mind that which conditions the specific dignity of the subject of the work. The activity of union organizations opens up many possibilities in this respect, including their *efforts to instruct and educate* the workers and to *foster their self-education*. Praise is due to the work of the schools, what are known as workers' or people's universities and the training programs and courses which have developed and are still developing this field of activity. It is always to be hoped that, thanks to the work of their unions, workers will not only *have* more, but above all *be* more: in other words, that they will realize their humanity more fully in every respect.

One method used by unions in pursuing the just rights of their members is *the strike* or work stoppage, as a kind of ultimatum to the competent bodies, especially the employers. This method is recognized by Catholic social teaching as legitimate in the proper conditions and within just limits. In this connection workers should be assured the *right to strike*, without being subjected to personal penal sanctions for taking part in a strike. While admitting that it is a legitimate means, we must at the same time emphasize that a strike remains, in a sense, an extreme means. *It must not be abused;* it must not be abused especially for "political" purposes. Furthermore it must never be forgotten that, when essential community services are in question, they must in every case be ensured, if necessary by means of appropriate legislation. Abuse of the strike weapon

50

can lead to the paralysis of the whole of socioeconomic life, and this is contrary to the requirements of the common good of society, which also corresponds to the properly understood nature of work itself.

21. Dignity of Agricultural Work

All that has been said thus far on the dignity of work, on the objective and subjective dimension of human work, can be directly applied to the question of agricultural work and to the situation of the person who cultivates the earth by toiling in the fields. This is a vast sector of work on our planet, a sector not restricted to one or another continent, nor limited to the societies which have already attained a certain level of development and progress. The world of agriculture, which provides society with the goods it needs for its daily sustenance, is of *fundamental importance.* The conditions of the rural population and of agricultural work vary from place to place, and the social position of agricultural workers differs from country to country. This depends not only on the level of development of agricultural technology but also, and perhaps more, on the recognition of the just rights of agricultural workers and, finally, on the level of awareness regarding the social ethics of work.

Agricultural work involves considerable difficulties, including unremitting and sometimes exhausting physical effort and a lack of appreciation on the part of society, to the point of making agricultural people feel that they are social outcasts and of speeding up the phenomenon of their mass exodus from the countryside to the cities and unfortunately to still more dehumanizing living conditions. Added to this are the lack of adequate professional training and of proper equipment, the spread of a certain individualism, and also *objectively unjust situations.* In certain developing countries, millions of people are forced to cultivate the land belonging to others and are exploited by the big landowners, without any hope of ever being able to gain possession of even a small piece of land of their own. There is a lack of forms of legal protection for the agricultural workers themselves and for their families in case of old age, sickness or unemployment. Long days of hard physical work are paid miserably. Land which could be cultivated is left abandoned by the owners. Legal titles to possession of a small portion of land that someone has personally cultivated for years are disregarded or left defenseless against the "land hunger" of more powerful individuals or groups. But even in the economically developed countries, where scientific research, technological achievements and State policy have brought agriculture to a very advanced level, the right to work can be infringed when the farm workers are denied the possibility of sharing in decisions concerning their services, or when they are denied the right to free association with a view to their just advancement socially, culturally and economically.

In many situations radical and urgent changes are therefore needed in order to restore to agriculture—and to rural people—their just value *as the basis for a healthy economy*, within the social community's development as a whole. Thus it is necessary to proclaim and promote the dignity of work, of all work but especially of agricultural work, in which man so eloquently "subdues" the earth he has received as a gift from God and affirms his "dominion" in the visible world.

22. The Disabled Person and Work

Recently, national communities and International Organizations have turned their attention to another question connected with work, one full of implications: the question of disabled people. They too are fully human subjects with corresponding innate, sacred and inviolable rights, and, in spite of the limitations and sufferings affecting their bodies and faculties, they point up more clearly the dignity and greatness of man. Since disabled people are subjects with all their rights, they should be helped to participate in the life of society in all its aspects and at all the levels accessible to their capacities. The disabled person is one of us and participates fully in the same humanity that we possess. It would be radically unworthy of man, and a denial of our common humanity, to admit to the life of the community, and thus admit to work, only those who are fully functional. To do so would be to practice *a serious form of discrimination*, that of the strong and healthy against the weak and sick. Work in the objective sense should be subordinated, in this circumstance too, to the dignity of man, to the subject of work and not to economic advantage.

The various bodies involved in the world of labor, both the direct and the indirect employer, should therefore by means of effective and appropriate measures foster the right of disabled people to professional training and work, so that they can be given a productive activity suited to them. Many practical problems arise at this point, as well as legal and economic ones; but the community, that is to say, the public authorities, associations and intermediate groups, business enterprises and the disabled themselves should pool their ideas and resources so as to attain this goal that must not be shirked: *that disabled people may be offered work according to their capabilities*, for this is demanded by their dignity as persons and as subjects of work. Each community will be able to set up suitable structures for finding or creating jobs for such people both in the usual public or private enterprises, by offering them ordinary or suitably adapted jobs, and in what are called "protected" enterprises and surroundings.

Careful attention must be devoted to the physical and psychological working conditions of disabled people—as for all workers—to their just remuneration, to the possibility of their promotion, and to the elimination of various obstacles. Without hiding the fact that this is a complex and difficult task, it is to be hoped that *a correct concept of labor in the subjective sense* will produce a situation which will make it possible for disabled people to feel that they are not cut off from the working world or dependent upon society, but that they are full-scale subjects of work, useful, respected for their human dignity and called to contribute to the progress and welfare of their families and of the community according to their particular capacities.

23. Work and the Emigration Question

Finally, we must say at least a few words on the subject of *emigration in search of work*. This is an age-old phenomenon which nevertheless continues to be repeated and is still today very widespread as a result of the complexities of modern life. Man has the right to leave his native land for various motives— and also the right to return—in order to seek better conditions of life in another country. This fact is certainly not without difficulties of various kinds. Above all it generally constitutes a loss for the country which is left behind. It is the departure of a person who is also a member of a great community united by history, tradition and culture; and that person must begin life in the midst of another society united by a different culture and very often by a different language. In this case, it is the loss of *a subject of work*, whose efforts of mind and body could contribute to the common good of his own country, but these efforts, this contribution, are instead offered to another society which in a sense has less right to them than the person's country of origin.

Nevertheless, even if emigration is in some aspects an evil, in certain circumstances it is, as the phrase goes, a necessary evil. Everything should be done—and certainly much is being done to this end—to prevent this material evil from causing greater *moral harm;* indeed every possible effort should be made to ensure that it may bring benefit to the emigrant's personal, family and social life, both for the country to which he goes and the country which he leaves. In this area much depends on just legislation, in particular with regard to the rights of workers. It is obvious that the question of just legislation enters into the context of the present considerations, especially from the point of view of these rights.

The most important thing is that the person working away from his native land, whether as a permanent emigrant or as a seasonal worker, should not be *placed at a disadvantage* in comparison with the other workers in that society in the matter of working rights. Emigration in search of work must in no way become an opportunity for financial or social exploitation. As regards the work relationship, the same criteria should

54

be applied to immigrant workers as to all other workers in the society concerned. The value of work should be measured by the same standard and not according to the difference in nationality, religion or race. For even greater reason the *situation of constraint* in which the emigrant may find himself *should not be exploited.* All these circumstances should categorically give way, after special qualifications have of course been taken into consideration, to the fundamental value of work, which is bound up with the dignity of the human person. Once more the fundamental principle must be repeated: the hierarchy of values and the profound meaning of work itself require that capital should be at the service of labor and not labor at the service of capital.

V

ELEMENTS FOR A SPIRITUALITY OF WORK

24. A Particular Task for the Church

It is right to devote the last part of these reflections about human work, on the occasion of the ninetieth anniversary of the Encyclical *Rerum novarum*, to the spirituality of work in the Christian sense. Since work in its subjective aspect is always a personal action, an *actus personae*, it follows that *the whole person, body and spirit*, participates in it, whether it is manual or intellectual work. It is also to the whole person that the word of the living God is directed, the evangelical message of salvation, in which we find many points which concern human work and which throw particular light on it. These points need to be properly assimilated: an inner effort on the part of the human spirit, guided by faith, hope and charity, is needed in order that through these points the *work* of the individual human being may *be given the meaning which it has in the eyes of God* and by means of which work enters into the salvation process on a par with the other ordinary yet particularly important components of its texture.

The Church considers it her duty to speak out on work from the viewpoint of its human value and of the moral order to which it belongs, and she sees this as one of her important tasks within the service that she renders to the evangelical message as a whole. At the same time she sees it as her particular duty *to form a spirituality of work* which will help all people to come closer, through work, to God, the Creator and Redeemer, to participate in His salvific plan for man and the world and to deepen their friendship with Christ in their lives

56

by accepting, through faith, a living participation in His three-fold mission as Priest, Prophet and King, as the Second Vatican Council so eloquently teaches.

25. Work as a Sharing in the Activity of the Creator

As the Second Vatican Council says, "throughout the course of the centuries, men have labored to better the circumstances of their lives through a monumental amount of individual and collective effort. To believers, this point is settled: considered in itself, such human activity accords with God's will. For man, created to God's image, received a mandate to subject to himself the earth and all that it contains, and to govern the world with justice and holiness; a mandate to relate himself and the totality of things to Him who was to be acknowledged as the Lord and Creator of all. Thus, by the subjection of all things to man, the name of God would be wonderful in all the earth."[27]

The word of God's revelation is profoundly marked by the fundamental truth that *man*, created in the image of God, *shares by his work in the activity of the Creator* and that, within the limits of his own human capabilities, man in a sense continues to develop that activity, and perfects it as he advances further and further in the discovery of the resources and values contained in the whole of creation. We find this truth at the very beginning of Sacred Scripture, in the book of Genesis, where the creation activity itself is presented in the form of "work" done by God during "six days,"[28] "resting" on the seventh day.[29] Besides, the last book of Sacred Scripture echoes the same respect for what God has done through His creative "work" when it proclaims: "Great and wonderful are your deeds, O Lord God the Almighty"[30]; this is similar to the book of Genesis, which concludes the description of each day of creation with the statement: "And God saw that it was good."[31]

This description of creation, which we find in the very first chapter of the book of Genesis, is also *in a sense the first "gospel of work."* For it shows what the dignity of work con-

57

sists of: it teaches that man ought to imitate God, his Creator, in working, because man alone has the unique characteristic of likeness to God. Man ought to imitate God both in working and also in resting, since God Himself wished to present His own creative activity under the form of *work and rest.* This activity by God in the world always continues, as the words of *Christ attest: "My Father is working still..."*[32]: He works with creative power by sustaining in existence the world that He called into being from nothing, and He works with salvific power in the hearts of those whom from the beginning He has destined for "rest"[33] in union with Himself in His "Father's house."[34] Therefore man's work too not only requires a rest every "seventh day,"[35] but also cannot consist in the mere exercise of human strength in external action; it must leave room for man to prepare himself, by becoming more and more what in the will of God he ought to be, for the *"rest" that the Lord reserves for His servants and friends.*[36]

Awareness that man's work is a participation in God's activity ought to permeate, as the Council teaches, even *"the most ordinary everyday activities.* For, while providing the substance of life for themselves and their families, men and women are performing their activities in a way which appropriately benefits society. They can justly consider that by their labor they are unfolding the Creator's work, consulting the advantages of their brothers and sisters, and contributing by their personal industry to the realization in history of the divine plan."[37]

This Christian spirituality of work should be a heritage shared by all. Especially in the modern age, the *spirituality* of work should show the *maturity* called for by the tensions and restlessness of mind and heart. "Far from thinking that works produced by man's own talent and energy are in opposition to God's power, and that the rational creature exists as a kind of rival to the Creator, Christians are convinced that the triumphs of the human race are a sign of God's greatness and the flowering of His own mysterious design. For the greater man's power becomes, the farther his individual and community responsibility extends. ...People are not deterred by *the Christian message* from building up the world, or impelled to neglect the welfare of their fellows. They are, rather, more stringently bound to do these very things."[38]

The knowledge that by means of work man shares in the work of creation constitutes the most profound *motive* for undertaking it in various sectors. "The faithful, therefore," we read in the Constitution *Lumen gentium*, "must learn the deepest meaning and the value of all creation, and its orientation to the praise of God. Even by their secular activity they must assist one another to live holier lives. In this way the world will be permeated by the spirit of Christ and more effectively achieve its purpose in justice, charity and peace.... Therefore, by their competence in secular fields and by their personal activity, elevated from within by the grace of Christ, let them work vigorously so that by human labor, technical skill, and civil culture created goods may be perfected according to the design of the Creator and the light of His Word."[39]

26. Christ, the Man of Work

The truth that by means of work man participates in the activity of God Himself, his Creator, was *given particular prominence by Jesus Christ*—the Jesus at whom many of His first listeners in Nazareth "were astonished, saying, 'Where did this man get all this? What is the wisdom given to him?... Is not this the carpenter?' "[40] For Jesus not only proclaimed but first and foremost fulfilled by His deeds the "gospel," the word of eternal Wisdom, that had been entrusted to Him. Therefore this was also "the gospel of work," because *He who proclaimed it was Himself a man of work*, a craftsman like Joseph of Nazareth.[41] And if we do not find in His words a special command to work—but rather on one occasion a prohibition against too much anxiety about work and life[42]—at the same time the eloquence of the life of Christ is unequivocal: He belongs to the "working world," He has appreciation and respect for human work. It can indeed be said that *He looks with love upon human work* and the different forms that it takes, seeing in each one of these forms a particular facet of man's likeness with God, the Creator and Father. Is it not He who says: "My Father is the vinedresser,"[43] and in various ways puts *into His teaching* the fundamental truth about work which is already expressed in the whole tradition of the Old Testament, beginning with the book of Genesis?

The books of the Old Testament contain many references to human work and to the individual professions exercised by man: for example, the doctor,[44] the pharmacist,[45] the craftsman or artist,[46] the blacksmith[47]—we could apply these words to today's foundry-workers—the potter,[48] the farmer,[49] the scholar,[50] the sailor,[51] the builder,[52] the musician,[53] the shepherd,[54] and the fisherman.[55] The words of praise for the work of women are well known.[56] *In His parables on the Kingdom* of God, Jesus Christ constantly refers to human work: that of the shepherd,[57] the farmer,[58] the doctor,[59] the sower,[60] the householder,[61] the servant,[62] the steward,[63] the fisherman,[64] the merchant,[65] the laborer.[66] He also speaks of the various forms of women's work.[67] He compares the apostolate to the manual work of harvesters[68] or fishermen.[69] He refers to the work of scholars too.[70]

This teaching of Christ on work, based on the example of His life during His years in Nazareth, finds a particularly lively echo *in the teaching of the Apostle Paul*. Paul boasts of working at his trade (he was probably a tent-maker),[71] and thanks to that work he was able even as an Apostle to earn his own bread.[72] "With toil and labor we worked night and day, that we might not burden any of you."[73] Hence his instructions, in the form of *exhortation and command*, on the subject of work: "Now such persons we command and exhort in the Lord Jesus Christ to do their work in quietness and to earn their own living," he writes to the Thessalonians.[74] In fact, noting that some "are living in idleness...not doing any work,"[75] the Apostle does not hesitate to say in the same context: "If any one will not work, let him not eat."[76] In another passage *he encourages* his readers: "Whatever your task, work heartily, as serving the Lord and not men, knowing that from the Lord you will receive the inheritance as your reward."[77]

The teachings of the Apostle of the Gentiles obviously have key importance for the morality and spirituality of human work. They are an important complement to the great though discreet gospel of work that we find in the life and parables of Christ, in what Jesus "did and taught."[78]

On the basis of these illuminations emanating from the Source Himself, the Church has always proclaimed what we find *expressed in modern terms* in the teaching of the Second Vatican Council: "Just as human activity proceeds from man, so it is ordered towards man. For when a man works he not only alters things and society, he develops himself as well. He learns much, he cultivates his resources, he goes outside of himself and beyond himself. Rightly understood, this kind of growth is of greater value than any external riches which can be garnered.... Hence, the norm of human activity is this: that in accord with the divine plan and will, it should harmonize with the genuine good of the human race, and allow people as individuals and as members of society to pursue their total vocation and fulfill it."[79]

Such a *vision of the values of human work*, or in other words such a spirituality of work, fully explains what we read in the same section of the Council's pastoral constitution with regard to the right *meaning of progress:* "A person is more precious for what he is than for what he has. Similarly, all that people do to obtain greater justice, wider brotherhood, and a more humane ordering of social relationships has greater worth than technical advances. For these advances can supply the material for human progress, but of themselves alone they can never actually bring it about."[80]

This teaching on the question of progress and development—a subject that dominates present-day thought—can be understood only as the fruit of a tested spirituality of human work; and it is *only on the basis of such a spirituality* that it can be realized and put into practice. This is the teaching, and also the program, that has its roots in "the gospel of work."

27. Human Work in the Light of the Cross and the Resurrection of Christ

There is yet another aspect of human work, an essential dimension of it, that is profoundly imbued with the spirituality based on the Gospel. All *work*, whether manual or intellectual, is inevitably linked with *toil*. The book of Genesis expresses it in a truly penetrating manner: the original *blessing* of work contained in the very mystery of creation and connected with man's elevation as the image of God is contrasted with the *curse* that *sin* brought with it: "Cursed is the ground because of you; in toil you shall eat of it all the days of your life."[81] This toil connected with work marks the way of human life on earth and constitutes *an announcement of death:* "In the sweat of your face you shall eat bread till you return to the ground, for out of it you were taken."[82] Almost as an echo of these words, the author of one of the Wisdom books says: "Then I considered all that my hands had done and the toil I had spent in doing it."[83] There is no one on earth who could not apply these words to himself.

In a sense, the final word of the Gospel on this matter as on others is found in the Paschal Mystery of Jesus Christ. It is here that we must seek an answer to these problems so important for the spirituality of human work. *The Paschal Mystery* contains *the Cross* of Christ and His obedience unto death, which the Apostle contrasts with the disobedience which from the beginning has burdened man's history on earth.[84] It also contains *the elevation* of Christ, who by means of death on a Cross returns to His disciples in *the Resurrection* with the power of the Holy Spirit.

Sweat and toil, which work necessarily involves in the present condition of the human race, present the Christian and everyone who is called to follow Christ with the possibility of sharing lovingly in the work that Christ came to do.[85] This work of salvation came about through suffering and death on a Cross. By enduring the toil of work in union with Christ crucified for us, man in a way collaborates with the Son of God for the redemption of humanity. He shows himself a true disciple of Christ by carrying the cross in his turn every day[86] in the activity that he is called upon to perform.

Christ, "undergoing death itself for all of us sinners, taught us by example that we too must shoulder that cross which the world and the flesh inflict upon those who pursue peace and justice"; but also, at the same time, "appointed Lord *by His Resurrection* and given all authority in heaven and on earth, Christ is now at work in people's hearts through the power of His Spirit.... He animates, purifies, and strengthens those noble longings too by which the human family strives *to make its life more human* and to render the whole earth submissive to this goal."[87]

The Christian finds in human work a small part of the Cross of Christ and accepts it in the same spirit of redemption in which Christ accepted His Cross for us. In work, thanks to the light that penetrates us from the Resurrection of Christ, we always find a *glimmer* of new life, of the *new good*, as if it were an announcement of "the new heavens and the new earth"[88] in which man and the world participate precisely through the toil that goes with work. Through toil—and never without it. On the one hand this confirms the indispensability of the Cross in the spirituality of human work; on the other hand the Cross which this toil constitutes reveals a new good springing from work itself, from work understood in depth and in all its aspects and never apart from work.

Is this *new good*—the fruit of human work—already a small part of that "new earth" where justice dwells?[89] If it is true that the many forms of toil that go with man's work are a small part of the Cross of Christ, what is the relationship of this new good to *the Resurrection of Christ?* The Council seeks to reply to this question also, drawing light from the very sources of the revealed word: "Therefore, while we are warned that it profits a man nothing if he gains the whole world and loses himself (cf. Lk. 9:25), the expectation of a new earth must not weaken but rather stimulate our concern for cultivating this one. For here grows the body of a new human family, a body which even now is able to give some kind of foreshadowing of the new age. Earthly progress must be carefully distinguished from the growth of Christ's Kingdom. Nevertheless, to the extent that the former can contribute to the better ordering of human society, it is of vital concern to the Kingdom of God."[90]

In these present reflections devoted to human work we have tried to emphasize everything that seemed essential to it, since it is through man's labor that not only "the fruits of our activity" but also "human dignity, brotherhood and freedom" must increase on earth.[91] Let the Christian who listens to the word of the living God, uniting work with prayer, know the place that his work has not only in *earthly progress* but also in *the development of the Kingdom of God,* to which we are all called through the power of the Holy Spirit and through the word of the Gospel.

In concluding these reflections, I gladly impart the Apostolic Blessing to all of you, venerable Brothers and beloved sons and daughters.

I prepared this document for publication on last May 15, on the ninetieth anniversary of the Encyclical *Rerum novarum,* but it is only after my stay in the hospital that I have been able to revise it definitively.

Given at Castel Gandolfo, on the fourteenth day of September, the Feast of the Triumph of the Cross, in the year 1981, the third of the Pontificate.

Joannes Paulus PP. II

Footnotes

1. Cf. Ps. 127(128):2; cf. also Gn. 3:17-19; Prv. 10:22; Ex. 1:8-14; Jer. 22:13.

2. Cf. Gn. 1:26.

3. Cf. Gn. 1:28.

4. Encyclical *Redemptor hominis*, no. 14: *AAS* 71 (1979), p. 284.

5. Cf. Ps. 127(128):2.

6. Gn. 3:19.

7. Cf. Mt. 13:52.

8. Second Vatican Ecumenical Council, Pastoral Constitution on the Church in the Modern World *Gaudium et spes*, no. 38: *AAS* 58 (1966), p. 1055.

9. Gn. 1:27.

10. Gn. 1:28.

11. Cf. Heb. 2:17; Phil. 2:5-8.

12. Cf. Pope Pius XI, Encyclical *Quadragesimo Anno: AAS* 23 (1931), p. 221.

13. Dt. 24:15; Jas. 5:4; and also Gn. 4:10.

14. Cf. Gn. 1:28.

15. Cf. Gn. 1:26-27.

16. Gn. 3:19.

17. Heb. 6:8; cf. Gn. 3:18.

18. Cf. *Summa Th.*, I-II, q. 40, a. 1, c.; I-II, q. 34, a. 2, ad 1.

19. Cf. *Summa Th.*, I-II, q. 40, a. 1, c.; I-II, q. 34, a. 2, ad 1.

20. Cf. Pope Pius XI, Encyclical *Quadragesimo Anno: AAS* 23 (1931), pp. 221-222.

21. Cf. Jn. 4:38.

22. On the right to property see *Summa Th.*, II-II, q. 66, arts. 2 and 6; *De Regimine Principum*, book 1, chapters 15 and 17. On the social function of property see *Summa Th.*, II-II, q. 134, art. 1, ad 3.

23. Cf. Pope Pius XI, Encyclical Quadragesimo Anno: AAS 23 (1931), p. 199; Second Vatican Ecumenical Council, Pastoral Constitution on the Church in the Modern World *Gaudium et spes*, no. 68: *AAS* 58 (1966), pp. 1089-1090.

24. Cf. Pope John XXIII, Encyclical *Mater et magistra: AAS* 53 (1961), p. 419.

25. Cf. *Summa Th.*, II-II, q. 65, a. 2.

26. Second Vatican Ecumenical Council, Pastoral Constitution on the Church in the Modern World *Gaudium et spes*, no. 67: *AAS* 58 (1966), p. 1089.

27. Second Vatican Ecumenical Council, Pastoral Constitution on the Church in the Modern World *Gaudium et spes*, no. 34: *AAS* 58 (1966), pp. 1052-1053.

28. Cf. Gn. 2:2; Ex. 20:8, 11; Dt. 5:12-14.

29. Cf. Gn. 2:3.

30. Rv. 15:3.

31. Gn. 1:4, 10, 12, 18, 21, 25, 31.

32. Jn. 5:17.

33. Cf. Heb. 4:1, 9-10.

34. Jn. 14:2.

35. Cf. Dt. 5:12-14; Ex. 20:8-12.

36. Cf. Mt. 25:21.

37. Second Vatican Ecumenical Council, Pastoral Constitution on the Church in the Modern World *Gaudium et spes*, no. 34: *AAS* 58 (1966), pp. 1052-1053.

38. *Ibid.*

39. Second Vatican Ecumenical Council, Dogmatic Constitution on the Church *Lumen gentium*, no. 36: *AAS* 57 (1965), p. 41.

40. Mk. 6:2-3.

41. Cf. Mt. 13:55.

42. Cf. Mt. 6:25-34.

43. Jn. 15:1.

44. Cf. Sir. 38:1-3.

45. Cf. Sir. 38:4-8.

46. Cf. Ex. 31:1-5; Sir. 38:27.

47. Cf. Gn. 4:22; Is. 44:12.

48. Cf. Jer. 18:3-4; Sir. 38:29-30.

49. Cf. Gn. 9:20; Is. 5:1-2.

50. Cf. Eccl. 12:9-12; Sir. 39:1-8.

51. Cf. Ps. 107(108):23-30; Wis. 14:2-3 a.

52. Cf. Gn. 11:3; 2 Kgs. 12:12-13; 22:5-6.

53. Cf. Gn. 4:21.

54. Cf. Gn. 4:2; 37:3; Ex. 3:1; 1 Sm. 16:11; et passim.

55. Cf. Ez. 47:10.

56. Cf. Prv. 31:15-27.

57. E.g. Jn. 10:1-16.

58. Cf. Mk. 12:1-12.

59. Cf. Lk. 4:23.

60. Cf. Mk. 4:1-9.

61. Cf. Mt. 13-52.

62. Cf. Mt. 24:45; Lk. 12:42-48.

63. Cf. Lk. 16:1-8.

64. Cf. Mt. 13:47-50.

65. Cf. Mt. 13:45-46.

66. Cf. Mt. 20:1-16.

67. Cf. Mt. 13:33; Lk. 15:8-9.

68. Cf. Mt. 9:37; Jn. 4:35-38.

69. Cf. Mt. 4:19.

70. Cf. Mt. 13:52.

71. Cf. Acts 18:3.

72. Cf. Acts 20:34-35.

73. 2 Thes. 3:8. St. Paul recognizes that missionaries have a right to their keep: 1 Cor. 9:6-14; Gal. 6:6; 2 Thes. 3:9; cf. Lk. 10:7.

74. 2 Thes. 3:12.

75. 2 Thes. 3:11.

76. 2 Thes. 3:10.

77. Col. 3:23-24.

78. Cf. Acts 1:1.

79. Second Vatican Ecumenical Council, Pastoral Constitution on the Church in the Modern World *Gaudium et spes*, no. 35: *AAS* 58 (1966), p. 1053.

80. *Ibid.*

81. Gn. 3:17.

82. Gn. 3:19.

83. Eccl. 2:11.

84. Cf. Rom. 5:19.

85. Cf. Jn. 17:4.

86. Cf. Lk. 9:23.

87. Second Vatican Ecumenical Council, Pastoral Constitution on the Church in the Modern World *Gaudium et spes*, no. 38: *AAS* 58 (1966), pp. 1055-1056.

88. Cf. 2 Pt. 3:13; Rv. 21:1.

89. Cf. 2 Pt. 3:13.

90. Second Vatican Ecumenical Council, Pastoral Constitution on the Church in the Modern World *Gaudium et spes*, no. 39: *AAS* 58 (1966), p. 1057.

91. *Ibid.*

═══ St. Paul Book & Media Centers ═══

ALASKA
750 West 5th Ave., Anchorage, AK 99501; 907-272-8183

CALIFORNIA
3908 Sepulveda Blvd., Culver City, CA 90230; 310-397-8676
5945 Balboa Ave., San Diego, CA 92111; 619-565-9181
46 Geary Street, San Francisco, CA 94108; 415-781-5180

FLORIDA
145 S.W. 107th Ave., Miami, FL 33174; 305-559-6715

HAWAII
1143 Bishop Street, Honolulu, HI 96813; 808-521-2731

ILLINOIS
172 North Michigan Ave., Chicago, IL 60601; 312-346-4228

LOUISIANA
4403 Veterans Memorial Blvd., Metairie, LA 70006; 504-887-7631

MASSACHUSETTS
50 St. Paul's Ave., Jamaica Plain, Boston, MA 02130; 617-522-8911
Rte. 1, 885 Providence Hwy., Dedham, MA 02026; 617-326-5385

MISSOURI
9804 Watson Rd., St. Louis, MO 63126; 314-965-3512

NEW JERSEY
561 U.S. Route 1, Wick Plaza, Edison, NJ 08817; 908-572-1200

NEW YORK
150 East 52nd Street, New York, NY 10022; 212-754-1110
78 Fort Place, Staten Island, NY 10301; 718-447-5071

OHIO
2105 Ontario Street, Cleveland, OH 44115; 216-621-9427

PENNSYLVANIA
214 W. DeKalb Pike, King of Prussia, PA 19406; 610-337-1882

SOUTH CAROLINA
243 King Street, Charleston, SC 29401; 803-577-0175

TENNESSEE
4811 Poplar Ave., Memphis, TN 38117; 901-761-0874

TEXAS
114 Main Plaza, San Antonio, TX 78205; 210-224-8101

VIRGINIA
1025 King Street, Alexandria, VA 22314; 703-549-3806

GUAM
285 Farenholt Avenue, Suite 308, Tamuning, Guam 96911; 671-646-7745

CANADA
3022 Dufferin Street, Toronto, Ontario, Canada M6B 3T5; 416-781-9131